Tarot Poems

By Christian Neill

[i] independents press
2023

[i] independents press
9451 35th Ave SW, Ste. 200
Seattle, WA 98126
ISBN 9-781312-304055
Printed in the USA by Lulu.com

Statement by the Author

The first time I touched a tarot deck, I was in middle school, and immediately sensed the power of what I held. It would be many years before re-approaching them with any seriousness. Several years ago, when deepening my tarot studies in earnest, I made an irregular practice of selecting a card at random and writing a poem about it. This was at first a way to deepen my understanding of the card and as a way to memorize meanings and symbolism. It also started cultivating my own relationships with the cards.

Over the years I put the poems and practice away, as I focused on doing more and more readings professionally. In reviewing my old notes, I rediscovered these recently, and thought it would be worth sharing some of them.

What follows is not intended to be authoritative or encyclopedic. The poems take different perspectives, have different relationships with the cards and symbolism, focus on different elements and take on different tones. They were each labors of love and engagement, and are proffered here as such. I hope you enjoy them and find in them some measure of invitation to go deeper.

Of course, these are only nineteen of the seventy-eight cards in a tarot deck, and every card contains volumes of poetry, insight, questioning and depth. Accept this modest contribution to the ongoing conversation around tarot, taking place in our culture today.

My sincere thanks and admiration to Pamela Coleman Smith and Arthur Waite for their pioneering work in bringing a venerable esoteric art to public consciousness. The card pictures are of the Smith-Waite tarot deck.

Key 16

Falling leaves like ashes
from a burning bush
perpetually consuming
transformation in destruction
as it so often goes
and upon these sacred heights a voice
cries out: this ground is not
stable. Or like snowflakes covering
the earth as if for sleep, to be
made new beneath
the death and dissolution, feeding
the promise of new life
after this too has passed and a new
sun has risen on this dark night.
What is this lightning break
that topples and sets aflame
the well-crafted misleadings of my heart,
that finds me in a tower and shows
me in a desert with nothing but a fall
headlong from my beloved heights (I had no idea
how high) accompanied by dead leaves
and dreams, trying as I go to embrace
the wind, the change, the new
foundationless, crownless, toppled, flaming
mass knowing a soft landing is too much
to hope, for the crash
skull splitting, unsurvivable (or so it seems),
but nights and fires and even death do not
last and though this blood
drained and dried on the well-trodden cliffs the sun
will rise (a greater fire, life-giving)
and my bones breathe again.

Two Swords

Trust is double-edged
when set upon by waves
and the unconscious sea
dimly lit as if by a slivered moon
and into one's open lap fall
two equally cutting
paths how to reach a distant
shore across a craggy unknown.
While these two blades rise
menacing, threatening
to cut the blindfold
from my eyes, could they,
those two deadly weapons
be fore this one reserved
and silent, blinded
would-be venturer still
seated, comforted by the weight
on my two shoulders
instead of deadly
weapons, merely
paddles?

KING ᴏғ WANDS

King of Fire

Is it strange that
vision clearest is focused
inward looking past
passions and desires in command,
creativity at hand,
almost in the act
of rising as if to take
change just then, just so
one's head on fire
with it all, determined
and determining, a lion
on his throne gazing
left as if something caught
attention, just out of sight
off-stage, in shadow,
but seen with urgency
nonetheless the way
a predator sees the whole hunt
before the first commanding
muscle twitch or
squint into the sun or future
master of all
he surveys and beyond
the empty hand holding
an invisible sword
a palpable power, if not quite
so explicit. The regal bearing
merely adornment,
the authority of a furrowed brow.

A Childhood Swordfight
Among Erstwhile Friends

Swinging from the middle
fighting myself and poor
position, as likely to trip
myself as hit my rival making
me all the more
angry and frustrated
there's just too much and
too many for me to get
a swing in, and this cocky
young thing crowing victory already
he hasn't even made a step yet
raising his stick in triumph
where I should be
in perfect position for striking but
not in the fight except
in his own imagination
(winning for all that).
Another whose caution is
tangling my blow awkward
on my shoulder still
as if he'd rather us all stop
before someone gets hurt
and watching the swinging
stick rather than the swinger,
he looking as if chopping wood
or striking ground than landing
a blow, and the fifth standing
open and wide-legged making
a ruckus but threatening no
real harm. Am I the only
one who cares about this
fight – the only one prepared to
injure (however ill-positioned)?
The only one absorbed with anger
on his face? Which makes this
all the more violent in me.

Not Satisfied with Insight

What did you expect, sitting
there legs and arms akimbo, staring
at your scarcity (a divine sum,
had you eyes to see) so intently
that even a gift of God out of seeming
nowhere escapes your notice
and the blessed portability
of an empty cup is lost
on you who'd rather sit
and not-quite-weep, not-quite-mourn,
refusing the solace of a certain
opinion or perspective, preferring to demure
rather than embrace either
the cold material or vaporish ephemeral
when there are trees to sit under,
thoughts to be mulled, universes to be
unraveled of one's own making,
moments to manufacture like a petulant
Buddha wrestling with Mara
and winning just enough to feel
ennobled (if not wise, but maybe),
or a proto-Newton waiting for an apple
to fall with immortality and importance, forgetting
all the while the chilling buttocks
on dewy grass and the huff
that drives away the subtle offering
on a wisp of cloud on a cloudless day.
An open eye is worth an insight now
and again.

Vista

Stretching out before me,
the ends of the earth
a low wrinkled link
thinly separating heaven
and beyond (as I know
the curvature of the planet provides
not end of horizons, but
this expanse is already
nearly unfathomable in its depth
and breadth), I stand not
as a master surveying,
more a boy leaving
his yard alone for the first
time – the possibilities almost
dizzying, the freedom in
simple choices or simply choosing
when the whole world seems equal:
destinations, adventure, promise,
and each footstep off a ledge
holding fast only
my desire, my passion, my creativity,
my hope, my daring, my foolishness
to steady me or be wielded
conquistador claiming a new land
merely by arriving, by standing
on new ground and declaring
I am here now
in this moment
all this is
forever mine.

Dark Knight of the Soul

Feet in the stirrup, ready
for battle, I find it rather appropriate
to wait, considering, surveying,
holding my earthly desires as if
in my hand for observation.
My dark steed beneath me strong and well-heeled,
crowned with mistletoe like horns
ready for charging or tender
kisses stolen under tradition's
indulgence of impolitic desires.
Over fertile fields ready for sowing
decisions difficult to undo
once shoulder has been put to plow
or yoke, the miracle of energy
transferred from food to muscle
to harness
and strap to plow to turnedover earth
and seed to food again
as if there were enough to think about and consider
even without the question to charge
or why and what
is to be hoped for or gained.
My own glistening armor reflecting
light from heaven itself against a backdrop
of illumination in the moment
of contemplation, consideration, alone
on that field prepared
for a harvest of one kind or another.
I wait, gazing at or through
my plans and consider which
way to pull the reins
as likely to turn and return
as to spur the present forward
lunge. But for now
all held as close as possibility
and my next breath.

(*untitled – The Magician*)

Hand raised in power or protest,
the other pointing here, no further,
girdled with a snake and infinity
overhead, the elements
and implements before you
on a table carved deep with sacred
symbols, secret, hidden,
surrounded by flowers.
Is that a hint of a smile
I detect on that young face
belying your years (or betraying
your lack thereof) wielding
power beyond yourself and yet
exactly the point,
the double-pointed beginning
of all that is is
in that moment, a conduit
between two worlds
two arcana
two secret powers and yet
so plainly known.
Drawing from what and sending
to where,
forming in what mystery
forgiving what mystery
the mystery
entirely aimed at understanding
and knowing just
that knowing isn't true
except when it is
roses above and roses below
the full flowering sense
of commonplace awe
and a magic of
beginning to connect
the wand with the hand.

(*untitled – The Fool*)

That oft-belabored fool for good
or for ill, perpetually one step from disaster
or flight, upon whom we heap
our hopes and our scorn;
bearer of our ideals, our jealousy, mystery.
What is that look on your face? upwards
toward the heavens surely but away
from the light, your satchel leaning
like a sunflower toward the sun;
even your red feather feels the gravity of light.
Yet it is not joy on your face,
not sorrow or pain, not longing or expectation
among those icy peaks, but almost
a look of sleep – not the world
of dreams but of one so focused
inward that their body is asleep and doesn't
matter.
The white rose thorns don't matter, except
to hold one's fingers tight.
I feel like the dog: awake but powerless
save for barking and hoping
to avoid disaster, tail up as if
perhaps this is just a game:
the heights, the sleep-walking,
light all around us without
eyes to see. Who is the fool?
The hound for hope? The page for dreaming?
The sun for wasting its rays? The icy
cliffs for bearing mute witness? Or
the precipice for daring to offer such
a view to one so unprepared to see
with eyes open the inevitable consequence
of one step after another
until almost all is lost.

(*untitled – The Hanged Man*)

In suspense, hanging
on a word, a future, the present
a past, my head aflame with seeing
the world turned
topmost-down, my hands are
bound powerless and unseen,
hanging by one foot fast, the other
free and crossing even
now going behind, finding
a different way
forming for some
the mirror of the Emperor
with all His control a prisoner
of convention, authority, rule,
and I for all outward captivity
am inwardly free
to see the truth,
die with my eyes open.

Open Sky

That youthful eye
and expression gazing,
mixture of awe and examination,
lifting gingerly yet up
to the light as if to see
the rainbow for the prism.
Eyes and horizon wide open,
nothing along but the object,
a blissfully unrecognized, uncomplicated freedom
to be nearly weightless
the buoyancy of fascination carrying,
setting off like a kite waiting
for a breeze in the cloudless sunshine
        in the meantime
hopes silently spreading like dandelions
underfoot, wildflowers beautiful
in their ubiquity, matter of fact,
more assumed than understood
when the difference escapes
gravity like seeds on the wind
to seed elsewhere anew
mountaintops and distant horizons to conquer
in good time, in good faith,
fertile fields between the future
and the verdant field that alights
the thoughts – waitless and heavy –
that delicious irony and contradiction
that is
a young person contemplating.

THE LOVERS.

The Lovers

That bridge between
understanding and
beauty, a choice that is
not one choice,
a lover, not one love,
Vesuvius rising beautiful
and threatening
molten heat from deep
pressure building
to bring rich soil.
Perhaps that is the fiery red hair
flames, arms, wings, sun itself outstretched
in embrace or extension
raising the trees of life and knowledge
or passing judgment,
the naked, hairless, smooth-skinned
ideals standing witness or accused
in their absurd naivete
given the choice, really,
who would stand palms out
and waiting at the foot of a volcano
whose gathering clouds forbode
that choice – to go
or stay, judge or embrace,
flee alone or risk together –
these two figures of fruit and flame,
no menace, no deceit,
only open-handed consideration
seeking balance
on unstable ground.

(untitled – Page of Wands)

A young woman heading
out for a first year
at art school, paint and brushes
in hand, at the ready,
the adventure of study, focus, creativity,
measuring the world by her ideals
and her thumb, flamboyant
as if her every movement, every garment,
       every day were a performance
a public beauty deeply personal
and playful
and serious
experimental and committed,
on a quest both inside and out,
one's growth tied to one's work tied
to one's growth in a mandala
of excellence, mastery, technique
to discover naivete, innocence, simplicity
of vision and insight
in a world still shaped by these
human hands
bringing to life as if by seeing ourselves more
clearly will bring its own
insight, own value.
On the edge of climbing
mountains or painting them.
Just at the beginning,
setting eyes
upward, full of hope
and critical sizing up,
noting the play of color, contrast,
light and distance
as only an artist can.
An artist already
and yearning yet to be.

THE WORLD.

(untitled – The World)

The dance is the dancer
in motion, in situ, in deed.
Naked, casting off
the protections of modesty,
       distance, armor, judgment
in the pirouette
creating one's own wind
in which to toss hair and glance,
wreathed in glory, victory
at the first faithful step,
be she surrounded by the world
in all its sinister and creative
possibilities, the clouded
witnesses each their own
outside the sacred circle
of her intention, attention,
       ascension,
candles burning at both ends,
the light of freedom holding nothing back,
three limbs raised in praise
to the almighty in
creation, the act of giving birth and being born
in that secret ovum,
the pressing space pressing
out, keeping out keeping
in integrating seeming dualities,
above below, inner outer,
whole and holy,
this world divided and broken
seeking and sought, brought
closer, closer
to one sheer moment
balanced on a turning toe.

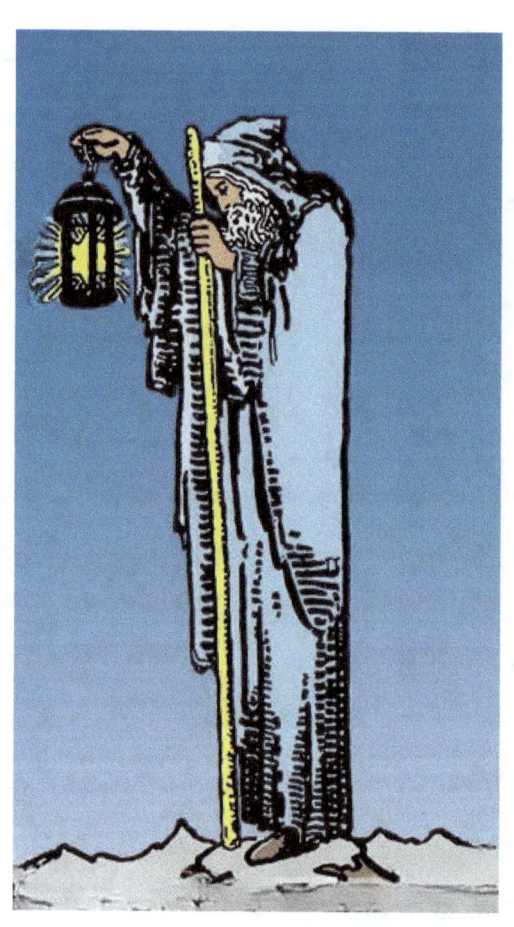

Nighttime Walk

Dark descends quickly after
sunset, when one loses
the way, sure footing, clear
sight forward and back
where one knows
where one knows
and walks unknowingly
content if one cares
to notice. The darkness
is tangible as the light gives
illusion there is
nothing to see
except the next stumbling
block. Focused so intently
searching for the next step
searching for the lights
searching for the way,
with one hand
steadying
a rod, and in the other
what you've been looking for
all along
to dispel the dark,
carrying your own illumination
and any next step
your path.

(untitled – Page of Cups)

The red-sleeved demon
of hope naively dancing
on the strand,
that in-between shore and sea looking
the other way
as if the rising waves held
no danger
and your feet both
salt and sand enough,
focused
eyes only
for the fish in your cup,
your golden portion
of the greater
sea
that cold faith too large
for even this holy grail.
A meeting of minds
made for the deep
captive on land
seeking a way back
to the Great
and either failing to see
or perhaps trusting
that all one needs
to do
is turn around,
and take a step.

(*untitled – The Hierophant*)

High holiness, a crown, a blessing,
a straight-forward gaze
between pillars of stone, occupying
the space between, the gap,
where we can only point
for what is not, the emptiness
among what solidly is
Grace
in a gesture
vested, elevated, honored
almost disappearing under the reverence.
Trinities abound:
three-tiered crown, and staff
(so far from a shepherd's crook),
supplicant, throne, and vault,
Father, Son and Spirit,
roses, lilies, and keys,
(desires, thoughts, and control;
body, soul, intention;
love, purity, daring),
two turned away, one toward
and expression neither of compassion
            or condemnation, but
what is
and raising blessing regardless
as if through time
handing down what has been
handed down
traditio
the one unclothed naked
skin able to see
know, feel
like steam escaping
a brief wisp ephemeral
from the gilded container
meant to hold,
transgresses, transmits, transitions
this one moment, to you.

Suppression

ropes bind me thick, corded, heavy
laid over me as if casually
tossed by an unthinking hand
pretending to not know
what the other
is doing
a convenient fiction that serves
its masters well and leaves
the parched earth cracked and peeling
still remembering floods and fertility
a fossilized dream that is beautiful
in its brokenness, a patterns of lightening
strikes preserved, each one special, unique,
but there are so many repeated

clouds so thick the sun is unwelcome
realizing the ropes
accepted unthinking beforehand
hands held back, magic between them

About the Author

Christian Neill is one of the most dynamic and trusted tarot readers in the Pacific Northwest. Serving as the official tarot reader of the King County Fair for several years, as well as teaching classes and doing professional readings in many contexts in Seattle, Christian has established himself as a go-to tarot reader. He offers a psychodynamic reading style that is akin to life-boarding, drawing on Jungian psychology, and years of training and experience in religious leadership and mental health. He lives and works in Seattle, and is currently working on a book presenting a revolutionary new way to engage tarot through the Kabbalah Tree of Life.